A LISTEN TO
Rock'N'Roll

Written by
Tom Greve

Rourke
Educational Media
rourkeeducationalmedia.com

Scan for Related Titles
and Teacher Resources

www.rourkeeducationalmedia.com

PHOTO CREDITS: Cover: © Simon Podgorsek; back cover, page 3, 4, 5: © dwphotos; page 1: © AAR Studio; page 6: © Bettmann/CORBIS; page 7: © oleg filipchuk (band), © Emilio Gelosi (sheet music); page 8: © kkgas; page 9: © Associated Press; page 10: © Jorge Delgado (guitar), © Brian Palmer (piano), © Sergey Dubrovskiy (drummer), © Marcin Pawlik (bass); page 11: Amy Nichole Harris (skyline), © Fritz Hiersche (musicians); page 13: © Liz Leyden (building), © Steve Kingsman (studio); page 14: © Nicole S. Young; page 15: © John Springer Collection/CORBIS; page 16: © Agnieszka Szymczak (skyline), © Derick A. Thomas; Dat's Jazz/CORBIS; page 17: © Ulrich Willmünder; page 18, 19: © Associated Press; page 20: © Steve Mandamadiotis (Tina Turner), © Brian Kushner (Patti Smith); page 21: © Kumax (Madonna), © GYI NSEA (Alisha Keys), © Christina71087 (Lady Gaga); page 22: © Lise Gagne

Edited by Precious McKenzie

Cover and Interior design by Tara Raymo

Library of Congress PCN Data

A Listen to Rock and Roll / Tom Greve
(Art and Music)
ISBN 978-1-62169-882-1 (hard cover)
ISBN 978-1-62169-777-0 (soft cover)
ISBN 978-1-62169-982-8 (e-Book)
Library of Congress Control Number: 2013936800

Also Available as:

Rourke Educational Media
Printed in the United States of America,
North Mankato, Minnesota

rourkeeducationalmedia.com

customerservice@rourkeeducationalmedia.com • PO Box 643328 Vero Beach, Florida 32964

Table of Contents

A Listen to Rock and Roll

Some forms of music move the imagination. Some forms of music can change a person's mood. Rock and roll music can do these things and more. It can make you want to move, dance, or shake. At its best, rock and roll chugs like a train on a rail.

Rock and roll music is art. Like drawing, storytelling, or dancing, it is for the enjoyment of the performer and the audience.

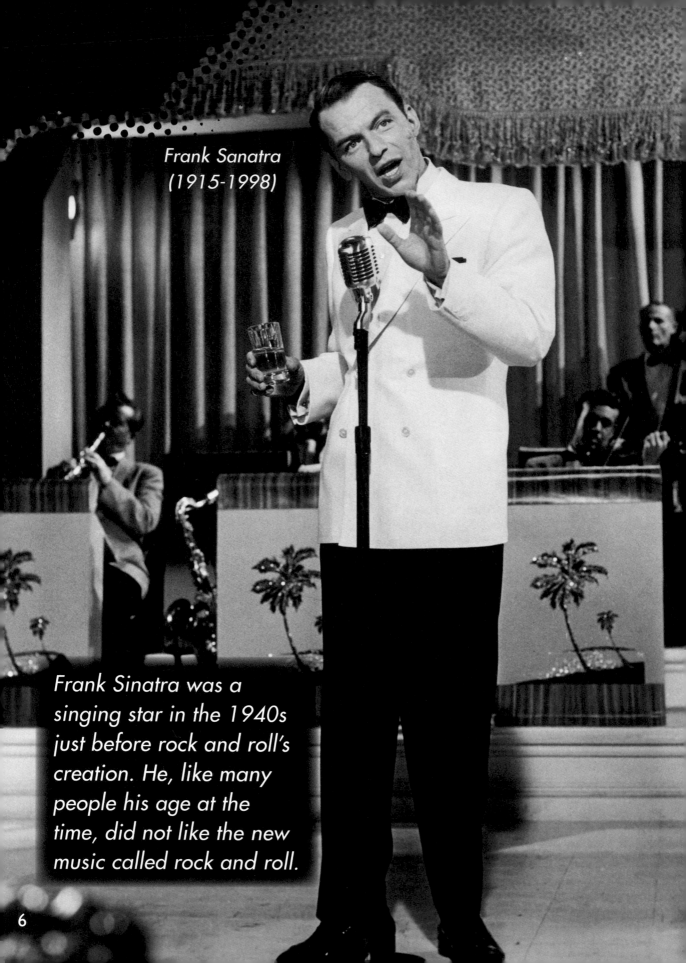

Frank Sanatra
(1915-1998)

Frank Sinatra was a singing star in the 1940s just before rock and roll's creation. He, like many people his age at the time, did not like the new music called rock and roll.

Rock and roll music is new. In fact, there are people alive today who can remember a time before there was rock and roll.

The creation of rock and roll music happened over several **generations**. It is the result of contributions from diverse **races**, **regions**, and musical **rebels**.

Rock and roll songs are usually short and played by just a few musicians in a band. Even the name is often shortened to rock n' roll, or just rock.

Races

Today's musicians still enjoy playing guitar blues songs.

In the early 1900s, African-Americans in the southern United States played blues and spiritual music. These were the first **ingredients** for what would become rock and roll.

BOB S BLUES

Robert Johnson played blues songs on guitar with repeating words and a simple song structure. His recordings from the 1930s influenced musicians a generation later and helped form rock and roll. He was just 27 when he died.

Spiritual music, with its emotional singing style,
was popular in southern African-American churches.

BLUES

Perfomed with voice and accoustic guitar

GOSPEL

Performed with voices and piano

RHYTHM AND BLUES

Performed with voice, guitar, piano, drums, and bass.

Mixing gospel and blues created a new kind of music called **rhythm** and blues. As recently as 1949, music magazines and radio stations called it race music since it was played almost exclusively by African-Americans.

Like blues and gospel, country music also influenced early rock and roll. Unlike blues and gospel, white musicians were playing and listening to country music in the first half of the 1900s.

Early country music utilized different stringed instruments like the banjo and the fiddle. While rock and roll's roots are in the south, Country music grew out of the rural, mountainous eastern part of Kentucky and Tennessee before gaining popularity in the city of Nashville.

Regions

The city of Memphis, Tennessee is where the blues of players like Robert Johnson, and the rhythm of gospel music came together into a new style known as rhythm and blues. It had a faster **tempo**, and a driving drum backbeat.

Rock and Roll Roots Map

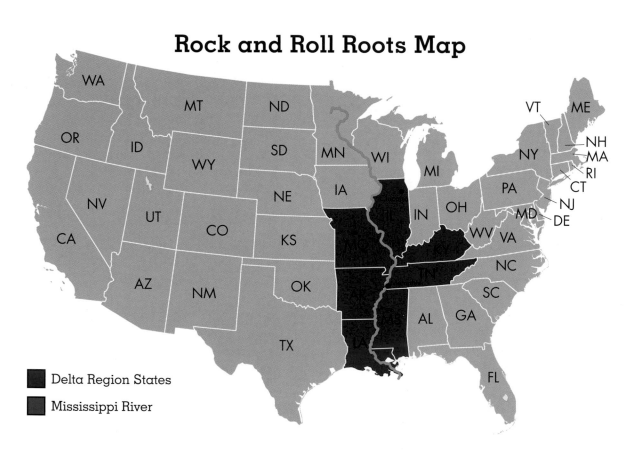

Delta Region States

Mississippi River

Rock and roll's roots are in the Delta region of Northwest Mississippi. By World War II, millions of African-Americans from Mississippi and other southern states had moved north to cities like Chicago, bringing the music with them.

SAM PHILLIPS
RHYTHM AND BLUES

Sam Phillips founded Memphis' Sun Studio. He recorded performances combining gospel rhythm and delta blues in the early 1950s. In 1951, he recorded a group of African-American musicians performing a song called *Rocket 88*. Nobody knew it at the time, but the song, with its fast blues style and drum beat, might be the first rock and roll song ever recorded.

Just a year after the recording of *Rocket 88*, a radio disc jockey named Alan Freed began calling rhythm and blues "rock and roll" music. By 1954, Sun Studio put out a record by a white performer named Elvis Presley. His musical performance style seemed new, but it was really just a new twist on Robert Johnson, Thomas Dorsey, and *Rocket 88*, all rolled together.

BACKBEAT BOOGIE

The secret to rock and roll may be its beat. Instead of simply keeping time for a melody, rock and roll uses a harder backbeat. With rock and roll, the simple pattern of bum, bum, bum became: boom-chicka-boom-chicka-boom- chicka-boom.

ELVIS

Elvis Presley's performance style made him not just famous, but dangerous! To many older people, Elvis' rock and roll music was too loud, too fast, and too crazy. Teenagers loved it even though most of their parents did not.

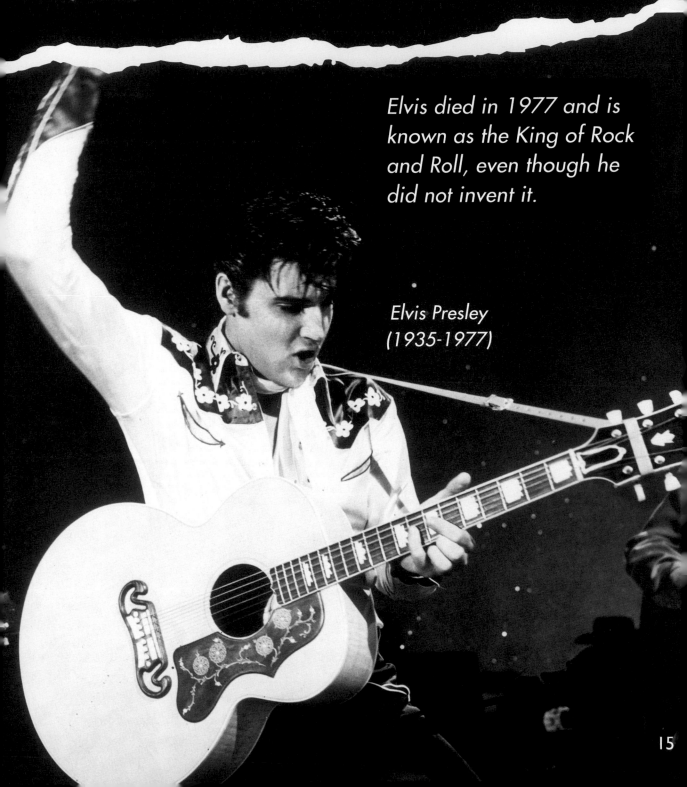

Elvis died in 1977 and is known as the King of Rock and Roll, even though he did not invent it.

Elvis Presley (1935-1977)

McKinley Morganfield was a southern delta blues player who moved north to Chicago around the time of World War II. Once in Chicago, he went by the name Muddy Waters.

McKinley Morganfield
(Muddy Waters 1913-1983)

In northern cities like Chicago, delta blues players used electric guitars to play louder in the crowded clubs. They played their blues with bands rather than alone.

With rock and roll now popular among American teenagers, the **urban** style of electric blues from Chicago soon found a young audience overseas in Great Britain. This started rock and roll's British Invasion!

British Invasion Map

■ Great Britain
■ United States

Rebels

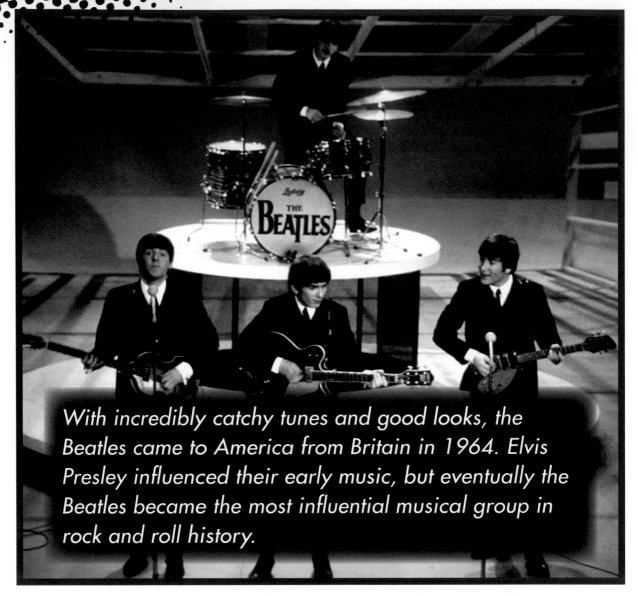

With incredibly catchy tunes and good looks, the Beatles came to America from Britain in 1964. Elvis Presley influenced their early music, but eventually the Beatles became the most influential musical group in rock and roll history.

By the early 1960s, rock and roll's fast, catchy music had many of the world's teenagers dancing, and grown-ups covering their ears. Elvis helped make rock and roll popular for young Americans, but British musicians made it popular all over the world.

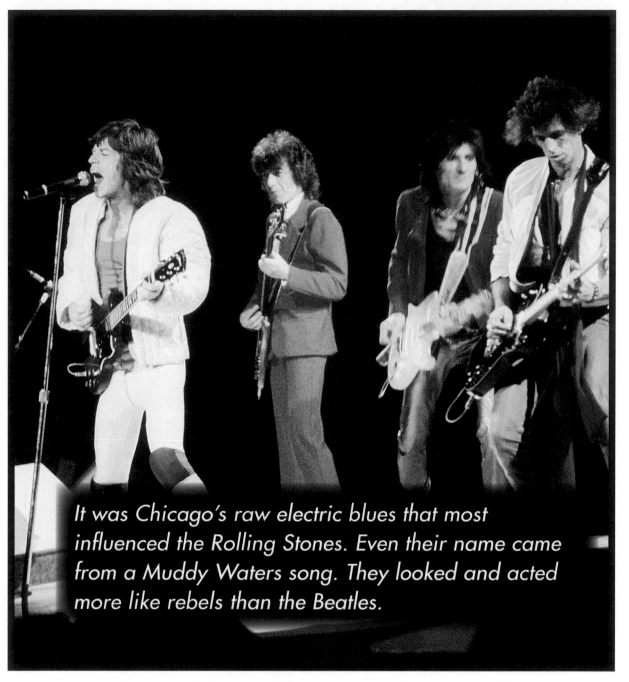

It was Chicago's raw electric blues that most influenced the Rolling Stones. Even their name came from a Muddy Waters song. They looked and acted more like rebels than the Beatles.

The Beatles and the Rolling Stones became the two most popular groups from the British Invasion. Each band's music remains popular to this day. Like the rhythm and blues musicians of the 1950s, their music let young people express themselves.

Since the British Invasion, rock and roll keeps shifting into other popular musical forms. Female performers have played big roles in these changes.

FEMALE PERFORMERS

Tina Turner gained fame in the late 60s and early 70s with a raw, bluesy singing style with her then-husband Ike Turner's band. Her fame quickly surpassed his, and she became one of rock and roll's top performers.

Patti Smith was a leader of the punk rock movement in the 1970s. Punk was an intense performance style of short, fast, simple songs.

Rock and roll is no longer the music of just teenagers. People of all ages listen to rock and roll and the pop music it has influenced. Each generation adds to, and changes, the music to express themselves and their times.

Madonna hit it big in the 1980s with her style of dancing and fashion. She has remained one of the world's biggest pop stars ever since.

Alicia Keys is a multi-talented singer, songwriter, and pianist from the rhythm and blues tradition of rock and roll. She is among the most popular current young performers.

Lady Gaga is an outrageous musician and performer. Her pop style, with its eye-popping fashion and dancing, is heavily influenced by Madonna.

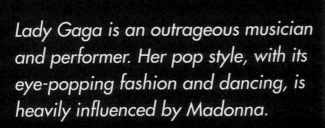

What began as rural, southern African-American music found its way to northern cities, and became a worldwide musical force delighting millions to this very day.

Since the British Invasion, rock and roll continues to influence new styles like punk, soul, new wave, heavy metal, grunge, rap, hip-hop, and other popular musical styles.

Glossary

generations (jen-uh-RAY-shuhnz): all people who are about the same ages

ingredients (in-GREE-dee-uhntz): individual items that something is made of

races (RAY-sez): the categorization of a group's ancestry or skin color

rebels (REB-uhlz): individuals who fight against the current system of doing something

regions (RE-juhnz): areas or specific parts of a state or country

rhythm (RITH-uhm): having a distinctive timing or pace

tempo (TEM-poh): the speed or timing of a piece of music

urban (UR-buhn): in the city

Index

Websites

www.Rockhall.com

www.sunstudio.com

www.BritishInvasionBands.com

About the Author

Tom Greve lives in Chicago with his wife and two kids. He is no longer a teenager, but he still loves listening to rock and roll and its many influences. He even plays a bit of guitar.

Meet The Author!
www.meetREMauthors.com